# FIVE
# MINUTE
# FINANCES

## *The Daily Habit That Can Change Your Life*

## By Tim Grimes

*For more information visit:*

# www.radicalcounselor.com

### Bulk purchases and speaking

*For discounts on bulk purchases, or to inquire about Tim speaking at your event, email <u>info@radicalcounselor.com</u>.*

ISBN-13: 978-1973969501
ISBN-10: 1973969505

Printed in the United States of America

# A personal message from Tim

Don't believe anything I say just at face value. Test it for yourself. If you test it, you'll see if it really works for you – or not. I feel confident that what I'm about to share with you will work, but don't listen to me. Listen to yourself.

# FIVE MINUTE FINANCES

I'm about to share with you a simple habit that can help improve your financial situation. It will only take up about five minutes of your day, and should reduce the anxiety you feel about money – while making more of it come into your life. It's an unusual habit in many ways, but one thing in particular stands out: *It's ridiculously easy.*

This habit is very undemanding, especially for those of us used to hearing complicated financial advice. You might laugh when you first hear it – or even get mad. You'll think, "That's it? Just doing that is going to help me feel better about money, and get more of it?"

Yet it's exactly *because* this financial advice is so unchallenging that it works.

This habit is simple, and you'll have no problem doing it over the long run, if you want. If you can brush your teeth every day, you can just as easily do this one small thing to improve your financial situation, which is welcome news for most of us.

So there's never any pressure with this habit. I'm a relaxed guy, and I focus on sharing relaxed advice. This isn't about making you into some kind of a special person, or pumping you up with a silly motivational tactic. Nor is it about making you rich. This habit isn't anything like that. It's just an unusual way to feel better about money, and gradually get more of it into your life.

In short, let's be easygoing about it. We don't get worked up about brushing our teeth, and there's no need to get worked up about this habit. But let me emphasize that it will probably seem weird to you at first.

The habit goes against the cultural norms we've been taught on how to be successful, and how we think we can improve our financial situation. If you don't feel comfortable going gently against the normal tide of thinking in terms of money, this habit probably isn't for you.

That said, there's nothing truly weird about it. Émile Coué, as well as several others, have already written extensively about the habit's effectiveness. This guide is intended as a quick summation of those longer explanations, with an emphasis put on your financial well-being. We're not going to be discussing any deep theory here. The point of this guide is to make this habit sound so easy that you feel like *you have to* test it out.

If you're wondering how long it will take to see results, the answer is almost always within three months. Positive things usually occur earlier – many of you will start feeling better about your finances immediately – and after a few months, it should become clear that this habit is helping to change your life for the better.

If three months sounds like a long time, I ask you to reconsider that assessment. Think about how many years people attend school to earn a degree, or learn something significant about a subject such as money. Consider the debt people accrue to go to graduate school, or to start a business. Likewise, think about how long many of us have been stressed out about money, and what that stress can do to our lives. Most of us have been stressed out about our financial situation – in some way or another – for a very long time.

What I'm getting at is that three months of doing something easy is not long, especially when it comes to money.

Imagine, just for a moment, that your financial stress wasn't there. Momentarily imagine having *no stress* over money…

It feels pretty good, right?

Well, I invite you to start feeling that sense of relief more regularly. The anxiety you feel about money doesn't usually need to be there, and following this simple routine will start eliminating it from your life. Regardless of its current level, your financial stress should lessen in the coming months. This habit is essentially too mechanical and automatic *not* to positively work for you in this way, as long as you consistently do it. I mean that. That's the power of it.

So let's get to the actual habit. This is the routine you should follow. I recommend initially not telling family or friends about what you're doing because, as I said, it sounds a bit odd. Just follow this routine daily. The habit is this one small thing, done each morning and evening. Here it is:

**For a few minutes upon waking in the morning, and before going to sleep at night, calmly repeat this phrase:** *"Every day, in every way, I'm getting wealthier and wealthier."*

And that's it. That's all you have to do.

Feel free to laugh. It's okay if the habit seems ridiculous to you. That doesn't matter. *Because it works.* Start repeating this phrase each morning and evening, and you'll soon see for yourself.

I'm intentionally not going to tell you *why* it works. Enough is already written on why this little habit is effective, but those longer explanations mean nothing if you don't do it for yourself. You'll find out if this works if you test it over the next few months – and not if you just read about it, think about it, or laugh at it.

*So just do it.*

It's very, very easy to follow this routine every day if you're intent upon improving your financial situation. You have little to lose, and a lot to potentially gain. I'll now briefly clear up some details so there's no confusion about the habit. Here it is once more:

**For a few minutes upon waking in the morning, and before going to sleep at night, calmly repeat this phrase:** *"Every day, in every way, I'm getting wealthier and wealthier."*

Again, I understand that just repeating this phrase to improve your financial situation seems absurd. I get where you're coming from. *But it also works.* And that's why I'm sharing it with you. I don't care how dumb, easy or juvenile it may sound. If you're serious about resolving money issues in your life, making this habit part of your daily routine will help you greatly.

Calmly repeat the phrase for a few minutes after waking up in the morning, and before going to sleep at night. Repeat it in a relaxed, methodical manner – feeling the subtle power of the words while you say it over and over again: *"Every day, in every way, I'm getting wealthier and wealthier…"*

It's best to do this in bed, resting comfortably, with your eyes closed. Repeat the phrase audibly, and be sure to move your lips; it's okay if you say it softy and produce only a faint whisper, as long as you can hear it.

Your thoughts might often run wild while you repeat *"Every day, in every way, I'm getting wealthier and wealthier."* Let them. No big deal. Just calmly keep repeating it with conviction. While repeating the phrase, especially at first, you might find yourself thinking things like, "This is absolutely the dumbest thing I've ever done, and I've done a lot of dumb things. This is the biggest waste of time ever. I'm an idiot."

That's fine. It doesn't matter. Let such thoughts go where they go. Happy thoughts, negative thoughts, whatever. This is mechanical. Often your thoughts will be all over the place while you quietly repeat the phrase. Just stay physically relaxed and keep repeating it for two or three minutes, regardless of the thoughts in your head. You can repeat it for much longer if you feel like it, but a few minutes is plenty if you don't want to repeat the phrase longer than that. Use a timer on your cell phone to keep track of time, if you wish.

Again, don't fight against your thoughts, and just faithfully repeat, *"Every day, in every way, I'm getting wealthier and wealthier..."* over and over again. Repeat it upon rising, and before you drift off at night. Do it habitually, relaxing in bed, and then go about living your normal life. You should soon start seeing results. It really *is* that simple.

Let me clarify why we say "wealthier," as opposed to saying something like "Every day, in every way, I'm getting more and more money." We use "wealthier" because feeling good usually has little to do with the actual amount of money we have. Wealth can imply richness in many different things, not just money: Friendships, family, health, material desires, finances, etc. It essentially means being satisfied.

So, becoming wealthier means fulfillment *"in every way"* possible, not just financially. The phrase *"Every day, in every way, I'm getting wealthier and wealthier"* signifies being satisfied with what you have now, and also satisfied with the natural, positive growth you're asserting in your life. "Money" is intentionally taken out of the equation, as there's a limit to what literal money can buy you, and the subject of "money" often inadvertently brings up negative connotations that "wealth" does not.

Actually, Émile Coué recommended a phrase that was even more general: *"Every day, in every way, I'm getting better and better."* You're welcome to use this phrase instead, but by replacing *"better"* with *"wealthier"* you can very gently focus on any perceived financial issues you have, as I know quite a few of you would like to do.

Repeating either phrase – *"Every day, in every way, I'm getting wealthier and wealthier"* or *"Every day, in every way, I'm getting better and better"* – will inevitably improve your relationship with money, and usually in a manner you never could have rationally conceived or planned.

Some of you are going to want to do more than just this one small thing each day. *But you don't need to.* Again, that's the beauty of it, and I can't emphasize it enough. This habit is easy and takes very little time. It's about as simple and stress-free as a daily exercise gets – like brushing your teeth. Repeating the phrase for a few minutes each morning and evening is enough to make it work. Then the rest of the day you can go about living your regular life.

As a matter of fact, trying to do more right out of the gate might prove *counterproductive.* Don't try unnaturally hard to improve things once you start following this new daily routine – make financial decisions that seem right to you and make sense, but let things happen at their own pace. Act normal. Allow your relationship with money to improve inwardly, at its own gradual speed – without worrying over what "needs" to be done next. In this way, the daily habit will easily ingrain itself into your lifestyle, with the least amount of stress involved.

And, with all that said, I still know that many of you will insist on doing *something* besides just this one habit. So, I'll give you a few optional exercises that complement it. But I must emphasize: *These other exercises are optional.* You only should do them if you want to. Otherwise, please don't bother, and just do the habit each morning and evening.

Here's the first complementary exercise you may find helpful:

*If you feel anxious or overwhelmed with negative thoughts, particularly about money, you can gently rub your forehead and quickly repeat (out loud) the phrase, "It passes, it passes, it passes..." over and over again until those negative feelings recede (which should usually be within a minute or two.)*

This exercise might sound even dumber than the habit itself. And guess what? It also works extremely well.

Why quickly repeat the phrase, *"it passes,"* over and over again when you find yourself getting anxious? Because it works! Let's not make simple things complicated! Audibly repeating, *"it passes,"* to yourself helps neutralize negative emotions, and exposes them for what they are – just passing thoughts and feelings. We can acknowledge those thoughts and feelings, and then let them pass at their own pace.

Most of us have subtle negative emotions associated with our financial situation (and some that aren't so subtle.) We often inadvertently think about money in a negative light, and mistakenly play into that negative emotional energy. It can be hard to actively battle against this. But there's no need to brood over our perceived financial problems for days, weeks, or months on end. What helps is noticing these negative thoughts and feelings about money when they show up, acknowledging them, and then *being okay* with letting them be there briefly.

None of these difficult thoughts and feelings have to turn into such a big deal. We don't have to belabor their existence. They're really not a big deal unless we make them one. There's nothing wrong with you just because some negative emotions are there. It's fine if they're there for a short period of time – whether it be for a few minutes, or many hours – and we don't have to wallow and beat ourselves up for feeling the way we do.

Repeating *"it passes"* helps stop that wallowing quickly. The phrase is easy to use. Lightly rubbing your forehead while saying it enables the process to work even faster. You can help offset the momentum of negative thoughts just by repeating the phrase quickly and rubbing your head. Less than a minute of quick repetition is usually enough time to begin neutralizing that wave of emotional energy. You notice it for what it is – just a flood of thoughts and feelings, and nothing necessarily more powerful or substantial than that. And then those negative emotions are less likely to seriously bother you, and can more easily be dismissed.

You can say *"it passes"* once, twice, or two hundred times in a row. Whatever. Repeat it when you feel it can help. But only say it when you *want* to say it – don't force it, and don't ever feel like you need to say it. Because you don't.

Another nice exercise that complements the daily habit is this:

*Close your eyes while sitting or standing still. Then calmly repeat the word "Wealth" over and over again.*

You can start saying *"Wealth"* more, if you want. It's a powerful word. Close your eyes, turn your focus inward, and repeat it softly for a minute or two. Rubbing your head, like in the last exercise, can be helpful here also.

You can perform this exercise after you have lunch, on the bus, before dinner, on the park bench, or whenever and wherever you like. You can repeat the word over and over again for several minutes – but even saying *"Wealth"* just a few times with gentle conviction can be effective. You can also choose to repeat it to yourself throughout the day, or write *"Wealth"* on a piece of paper that you keep in your pocket and look at occasionally.

None of these exercises are meant as overtly positive affirmations. They're not meant to pump you up (or trick yourself) into getting positive about having money you don't have. Affirmations like this often involve too much continual effort, and therefore are quite likely to fail over the long run.

I'm simply suggesting that you can utilize a word such as *"Wealth"* – or a similarly powerful word you like, such as *"Peace," "Calm," "Love," "Perfect," "Free,"*

*"Strong,"* etc. – throughout the day, whenever you want. It's a new verbal anchor you've created to help calm down, neutralize negative feelings, become present, and feel the abundance that's *already* inherent within you.

Because of this, you can rely on powerful words like this rather methodically. *"Wealth"* implies a sense of fulfillment and ease with the present moment. It's the kind of word that lets you know there's nothing that literally needs to be done in this moment besides what's happening, and everything is actually fine as it is. Repeating a word like that, using it as an anchor, helps you become less reactive to negative thoughts, while allowing uncomfortable feelings to fall off your shoulders faster.

If you prefer, you can also say something like, *"I'm wealthy"* over and over again, or a similar "I am" phrase. But you don't need to personalize what you're repeating by putting "I am" in front of it unless you like doing that – it's not necessary. Sometimes you might prefer repeating *"Wealth,"* while sometimes you might prefer to repeat, *"I'm wealthy."* And sometimes you might not feel like saying anything at all. As always, do what feels best for you in that moment.

So those are some complementary exercises. But they're all unnecessary unless you feel like doing them. What *is* necessary is the one foundational habit:

**For a few minutes upon waking in the morning, and before going to sleep at night, calmly repeat this phrase:** *"Every day, in every way, I'm getting wealthier and wealthier."*

Do it every day, in the morning and evening. (Or repeat, *"Every day, in every way, I'm getting better and better."*) This habit hardly takes any time – only about five minutes of your day, unless you feel like doing it for longer. Many of you will quickly start feeling better by doing it, and some of you will see fast financial improvements as well. But this isn't about rapid financial results.

*It's about changing your relationship with money for the rest of your life.*

Over time, this simple habit makes your relationship with money considerably less stressful. It naturally helps improve that relationship. So be patient with yourself and let the habit gradually work its "magic." Don't be concerned if you don't see any external results within the first week or two, or even within the first six to ten weeks. This isn't about making a quick buck. It's more profound, and its reach extends much further if done consistently over time.

Usually, if we're looking for big changes in our lives, they take time to develop. It's rare that they miraculously happen in a month or two (although they can). So please don't put any pressure on yourself. If anything, do the opposite: *Relax, do the simple habit every day, and don't worry about your financial future.* Go about living life normally. Let pleasant feelings of increased self-worth be your first signs of success, and consider any other initial outer changes as added bonuses.

The big outer changes do eventually come, sooner or later. Often, it's sooner than we expect. Progressively, as those weeks turn into months – and even later, if you allow those months to become years – that inner wealth builds up. Your daily habit leads to *exponential* external improvement, if given time. So use patience. How much money you have – as well as your entire sense of personal abundance – can be transformed by *"Every day, in every way, I'm getting wealthier and wealthier…"*

That's the big picture. I feel confident you'll begin seeing and experiencing it for yourself very soon. Until then, please let me know if you have any questions. Cheers to your inherent wealth.

# Speeches & Workshops

## *Five Minute Finances*
## Keynote or Workshop

**Tim Grimes** *speaks authoritatively on topics centered around stress relief, work-life balance and personal fulfillment. Based upon his unique background and experience, Tim shares surprising ways for everyone to become more productive and fulfilled by embracing relaxation as a paradigm for success.*

To inquire about Tim speaking
at your next event, email:
*info@radicalcounselor.com*

*For more information visit:*

# www.radicalcounselor.com

Printed in Great Britain
by Amazon

78127359R00021